ANIMALS
& INSTRUMENTS

WORLD TOUR

FUN-SCHOOLING JOURNAL

Language Arts, Geography,
Science & Music

Created By:
Linda Janisse & Sue Gerdes

Illustrations By:
Anna Kidalova, Tristan Mark
Miss Bianca & Linda Janisse

Cover & Design Work:
Sarah Janisse Brown

FunSchooling.com

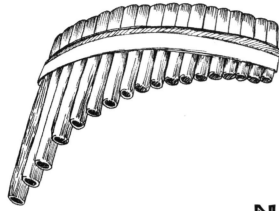

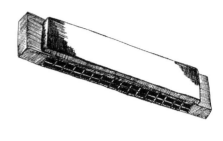

NAME:

DATE:

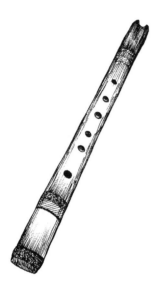

Age:

Contact Information:

ABOUT THE WORLD TOUR FUN-SCHOOLING JOURNAL:

This **285** page journal is designed for homeschoolers interested in Music, Travel & Animals! It covers several required subjects while focusing on the student's passion. The student will work through this learning handbook using resources from the Internet, local library and family bookshelf. The World Tour Fun-Schooling Journal is perfect for students of all abilities, ages **10+**, or younger with assistance. The book includes geography, history, animal research, art, spelling, language arts, cursive, folklore, fashion, food and more! A student can approach learning as a whole, while studying with this well rounded curriculum. Students will be challenged with different research prompts and explore their own creative interests.

Thinking Tree Learning Levels: **B2, C1 & C2**, ideal for ages **10+** (even adults!), younger children with assistance.

You might have met these animals and instruments in *Spelling Time*. Imagine that your favorite animal musicians have cousins. Their cousins play the same Instrument, but they live somewhere else. We will be digging deeper, traveling farther, and adding more fun to this learning journey!

INSTRUCTIONS:

To complete this guided learning journal students need access to library books, maps, Google Earth, Encyclopedias or online research tools and films/documentaries easily found online.

150+ SPELLING & VOCABULARY WORDS

Aardvark
Accordion
Adam
Awesome
Australia
Banjo
Bear
Brazil
Benjamin
Bodacious
Croatia
Cat
Courageous
Casey
Cowbell
Daniel
Dauntless
Djembe
Denmark
Dog
Ethiopia
Elephant
Ezra
Erhu
Empathetic
Fiddle
Faith
Fox
Fiji
Fashionable
Gregarious
Giraffe
Gwenevere
Gambia
Guitar
Hamster
Happy
Harmonica
Harmonie
Hungary

Iguana
Inci
India
Idealistic
Ivan
Jaguar
Jamaica
James
Jovial
Jug
Kangaroo
Kazoo
Kailani
Kind
Kazakhstan
Lithuania
Lion
Lawful
Lincoln
Lute
Mandolin
Miguel
Mellow
Monkey
Morocco
Noah
Nimble
Ney
Norway
Nutria
Oboe
Odessa
Opossum
Obliging
Oliver
Pan Pipes
Panda
Peter
Peaceful
Peru

Quebec City
Quena
Quizzical
Quiana
Quokka
Raccoon
Ruben
Recorder
Roving
Rwanda
Sergio
Saxophone
Sensitive
Skunk
Spain
Thoughtful
Tambourine
Turkey
Tiger
Tallulah
Uakari
Uruguay
Ukulele
Unselfish
Ulises
Vociferous
Veda
Vicuna
Venezuela
Volynka
Wilmina
Wolfsburg
Washtub bass
Wolf
Warmhearted
Xai-Xai
Xander
Xenodochial
Xerus
Xylophone

Yak
Yichang
Yuri
Yielding
Yunluo
Zeke
Zestful
Zebra
Zambia
Zither

VERBS:

Accompany
Brandish
Captivate
Differentiate
Encourage
Fascinate
Generate
Harmonize
Illuminate
Journey
Kindle
Launch
Measure
Negotiate
Originate
Postulate
Qualify
Recommend
Sentimentalize
Thrive
Undergo
Venerate
Welcome
Xerox
Yearn
Zip

ADAM THE AWESOME AARDVARK
PLAYS THE ACCORDION IN AUSTRALIA

Take some time to color and design the background for each picture while listening to music!

Doing this will help you to remember everything you are learning in this book.
You are encouraged to use your imagination and have fun!!!

MEET THE AARDVARK

Where do I live?

_____

_____

What do I eat?

My scientific name:

_____

_____

_____

_____

Describe my home/habitat and behavior.

_____

_____

_____

_____

_____

_____

_____

Write about my history or folklore.

_____

_____

_____

_____

_____

_____

ALL ABOUT THE ACCORDION

Describe this instrument.

_____

_____

_____

_____

_____

_____

Meaning of its name:

_____

_____

When, where, and by whom was it invented?

_____

_____

_____

_____

How do you play this instrument?

_____

_____

_____

Who is famous for playing this instrument?

_____

_____

_____

_____

AUSTRALIA

Color this location on the map:

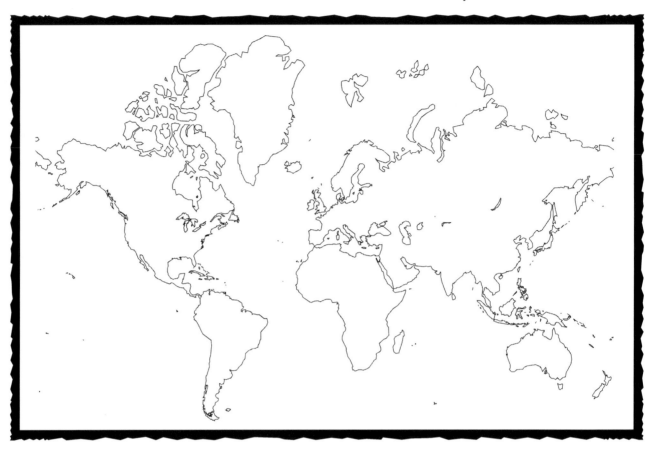

How far do you have to travel to reach this destination?
How would you get there?
What is the cost of travel to this location?
What is the currency called?
What is the current exchange rate?
What language is spoken there?
What is the weather like right now in this location?
What would you pack for this trip?

WRITE, DRAW OR PASTE A PHOTO

Flag	Popular Food
Current Events	**Famous Landmark**
A Famous Person	**A Postage Stamp**

TRY A TRADITIONAL RECIPE

Ingredients:

_____
_____
_____
_____
_____
_____
_____
_____
_____
_____
_____
_____
_____
_____
_____
_____
_____
_____

Prep Time:

Oven Temp:

Cook Time:

Directions:

_____
_____
_____
_____
_____
_____
_____
_____
_____
_____
_____
_____
_____
_____
_____
_____

Draw a picture or paste a photo of your culinary masterpiece here

SPELLING AND VOCABULARY CHALLENGE

In each section, you will be collecting new spelling words to define and learn. We will get you started with the first two. While doing your research, look for eight interesting words that you do not already know. Jot them down on the spelling list provided in each section as you go along.

FIND & DEFINE 10 NEW SPELLING WORDS
WRITE THEIR DEFINITIONS:

1. Awesome_____

_____

2. Accompany_____

_____

3._____

_____

4._____

_____

5._____

_____

6._____

_____

7._____

_____

8._____

_____

9._____

_____

10._____

_____

CURSIVE PRACTICE

Copy the words on this page.
Use the next page to write
your spelling words in cursive.

Adam

awesome

aardvark

plays

the

accordian

in

Australia

Cursive Practice

A B C D E F G

H I J K L M

N O P Q R S T

U V W X Y Z

a b c d e f g h

i j k l m n o p

q r s t u v w x

y z 1 2 3 4 5 6 7 8 9 0

BENJAMIN THE BODACIOUS BEAR PLAYS THE BANJO IN BRAZIL

MEET THE BEAR

My scientific name:

Where do I live?

What do I eat?

Describe my home/habitat and behavior.

Write about my history or folklore.

ALL ABOUT THE BANJO

Describe this instrument.

_____

_____

_____

_____

_____

_____

Meaning of its name:

_____

_____

When, where, and by whom was it invented?

_____

_____

_____

_____

How do you play this instrument?

_____

_____

_____

_____

Who is famous for playing this instrument?

_____

_____

_____

_____

BRAZIL

Color this location on the map:

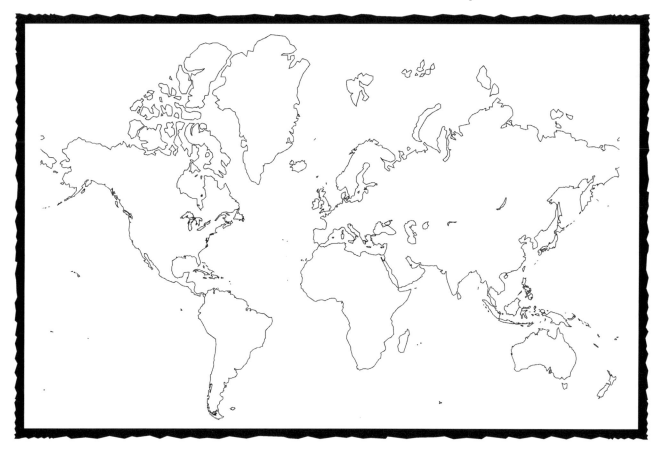

How far do you have to travel to reach this destination?
How would you get there?
What is the cost of travel to this location?
What is the currency called?
What is the current exchange rate?
What language is spoken there?
What is the weather like right now in this location?
What would you pack for this trip?

WRITE, DRAW OR PASTE A PHOTO

Flag	Popular Food
Current Events	**Famous Landmark**
A Famous Person	**A Postage Stamp**

WRITE A SHORT STORY, SONG, OR POEM
USING THESE WORDS:

Benjamin   Bear   Banjo
Brazil   Bodacious   Brandish

Title: Date:

_____

_____

_____

_____

_____

_____

_____

_____

_____

_____

_____

_____

_____

Illustrate your story, song, or poem here

FROM YOUR RESEARCH,
FIND & DEFINE 10 NEW SPELLING WORDS

1. bodacious _____

_____

2. brandish _____

_____

3. _____

_____

4. _____

_____

5. _____

_____

6. _____

_____

7. _____

_____

8. _____

_____

9. _____

_____

10. _____

_____

CURSIVE PRACTICE

Copy the words on this page.
Use the next page to write
your spelling words in cursive.

Benjamin

bodacious

bear

plays

the

banjo

in

Brazil

FILM STUDY

Find a video about the animal, instrument, or place. Draw something from the video and share what you learned in the space provided below.

Name of Video: _____

Notes:

_____
_____
_____
_____
_____
_____
_____
_____
_____

CASEY THE COURAGEOUS CAT PLAYS THE COWBELL IN CROATIA

MEET THE CAT

My scientific name:

_____

Where do I live?

_____

_____

What do I eat?

_____

_____

_____

Describe my home/habitat and behavior.

_____

_____

_____

_____

_____

_____

_____

_____

Write about my history or folklore.

_____

_____

_____

_____

_____

_____

ALL ABOUT THE COWBELL

Describe this instrument.

_____

_____

_____

_____

_____

_____

Meaning of its name:

_____

_____

When, where, and by whom was it invented?

_____

_____

_____

_____

How do you play this instrument?

_____

_____

_____

_____

Who is famous for playing this instrument?

_____

_____

_____

_____

CROATIA

Color this location on the map:

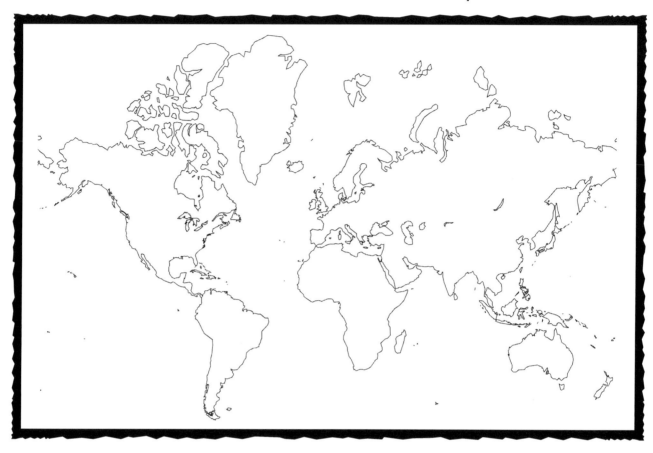

How far do you have to travel to reach this destination?
How would you get there?
What is the cost of travel to this location?
What is the currency called?
What is the current exchange rate?
What language is spoken there?
What is the weather like right now in this location?
What would you pack for this trip?

WRITE, DRAW OR PASTE A PHOTO

Flag	Popular Food

Current Events	Famous Landmark

A Famous Person	A Postage Stamp

DRAW OR PASTE PHOTOS OF TRADITIONAL CLOTHING

FROM YOUR RESEARCH,
FIND & DEFINE 10 NEW SPELLING WORDS

1. courageous_____

_____

2. captivate_____

_____

3._____

_____

4._____

_____

5._____

_____

6._____

_____

7._____

_____

8._____

_____

9._____

_____

10._____

_____

CURSIVE PRACTICE

Copy the words on this page.
Use the next page to write
your spelling words in cursive.

Casey

courageous

cat

plays

the

cowbell

in

Croatia

FILM STUDY

Find a video about the animal, instrument, or place.
Draw something from the video and share what you learned
in the space provided below.

Name of Video: _____

Notes:

_____

_____

_____

_____

_____

_____

_____

_____

DANIEL THE DAUNTLESS DOG PLAYS
THE DJEMBE IN DENMARK

MEET THE DOG

My scientific name:

_____

Where do I live?

_____

_____

What do I eat?

_____

_____

_____

Describe my home/habitat and behavior.

_____

_____

_____

_____

_____

_____

_____

Write about my history or folklore.

_____

_____

_____

_____

_____

ALL ABOUT THE DJEMBE

Describe this instrument.

_____
_____
_____
_____
_____
_____
_____

Meaning of its name:

_____
_____

When, where, and by whom was it invented?

_____
_____
_____
_____

How do you play this instrument?

_____
_____
_____

Who is famous for playing this instrument?

_____
_____
_____
_____

DENMARK

Color this location on the map:

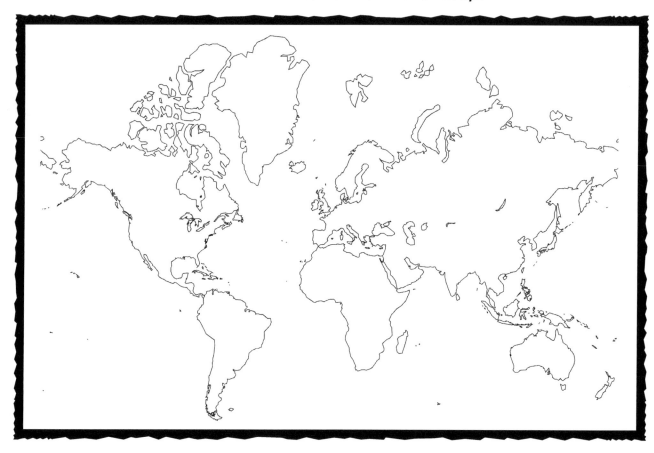

How far do you have to travel to reach this destination?
How would you get there?
What is the cost of travel to this location?
What is the currency called?
What is the current exchange rate?
What language is spoken there?
What is the weather like right now in this location?
What would you pack for this trip?

WRITE, DRAW OR PASTE A PHOTO

Flag	Popular Food
Current Events	**Famous Landmark**
A Famous Person	**A Postage Stamp**

TRY A TRADITIONAL RECIPE

Ingredients:

_____
_____
_____
_____
_____
_____
_____
_____
_____
_____
_____
_____
_____
_____
_____
_____
_____
_____
_____

Prep Time:

Oven Temp:

Cook Time:

Directions:

_____
_____
_____
_____
_____
_____
_____
_____
_____
_____
_____
_____
_____
_____
_____
_____

Draw a picture or paste a photo of your culinary masterpiece here

FROM YOUR RESEARCH,
FIND & DEFINE 10 NEW SPELLING WORDS

1. dauntless _____

_____

2. differentiate _____

_____

3. _____

_____

4. _____

_____

5. _____

_____

6. _____

_____

7. _____

_____

8. _____

_____

9. _____

_____

10. _____

_____

CURSIVE PRACTICE

Copy the words on this page.
Use the next page to write
your spelling words in cursive.

Daniel

dauntless

dog

plays

the

djembe

in

Denmark

44

WRITE A SHORT STORY, SONG, OR POEM USING THESE WORDS:

Daniel   Dog   Djembe
Denmark   Dauntless   Differentiate

Title: _____   Date: _____

_____

_____

_____

_____

_____

_____

_____

_____

_____

_____

_____

_____

illustrate your story, song, or poem here

ELIJAH THE EMPATHETIC ELEPHANT PLAYS THE ERHU IN ETHIOPIA

MEET THE ELEPHANT

My scientific name:

_____

Where do I live?

_____

_____

What do I eat?

_____

_____

_____

Describe my home/habitat and behavior.

_____

_____

_____

_____

_____

_____

_____

Write about my history or folklore.

_____

_____

_____

_____

_____

ALL ABOUT THE EHRU

Describe this instrument.

_____

_____

_____

_____

_____

_____

_____

Meaning of its name:

_____

_____

When, where, and by whom was it invented?

_____

_____

_____

_____

How do you play this instrument?

_____

_____

_____

Who is famous for playing this instrument?

_____

_____

_____

_____

ETHIOPIA

Color this location on the map:

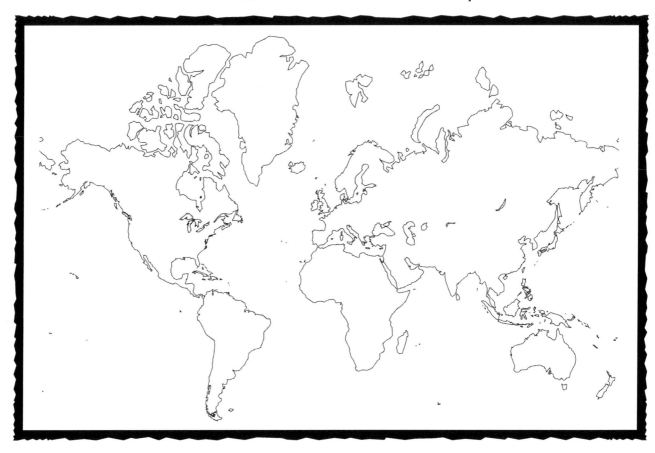

How far do you have to travel to reach this destination?
How would you get there?
What is the cost of travel to this location?
What is the currency called?
What is the current exchange rate?
What language is spoken there?
What is the weather like right now in this location?
What would you pack for this trip?

WRITE, DRAW OR PASTE A PHOTO

Flag	Popular Food

Current Events	Famous Landmark

A Famous Person	A Postage Stamp

DRAW OR PASTE PHOTOS OF TRADITIONAL CLOTHING

FROM YOUR RESEARCH,
FIND & DEFINE 10 NEW SPELLING WORDS

1. empathetic_____

_____

2. encourage_____

_____

3._____

_____

4._____

_____

5._____

_____

6._____

_____

7._____

_____

8._____

_____

9._____

_____

10._____

_____

CURSIVE PRACTICE

Copy the words on this page.
Use the next page to write
your spelling words in cursive.

Ezra

empathetic

elephant

plays

the

erhu

in

Ethiopia

FILM STUDY

Find a video about the animal, instrument, or place. Draw something from the video and share what you learned in the space provided below.

Name of Video: _____

Notes:

_____

_____

_____

_____

_____

_____

_____

_____

_____

FAITH THE FASHIONABLE FOX PLAYS THE FIDDLE IN FIJI

MEET THE FOX

My scientific name:

_____

Where do I live?

_____

_____

What do I eat?

_____

_____

_____

Describe my home/habitat and behavior.

_____

_____

_____

_____

_____

_____

_____

_____

Write about my history or folklore.

_____

_____

_____

_____

_____

ALL ABOUT THE FIDDLE

Describe this instrument.

_____
_____
_____
_____
_____
_____
_____

Meaning of its name:

_____
_____

When, where, and by whom was it invented?

_____
_____
_____
_____

How do you play this instrument?

_____
_____
_____

Who is famous for playing this instrument?

_____
_____
_____
_____

FIJI

Color this location on the map:

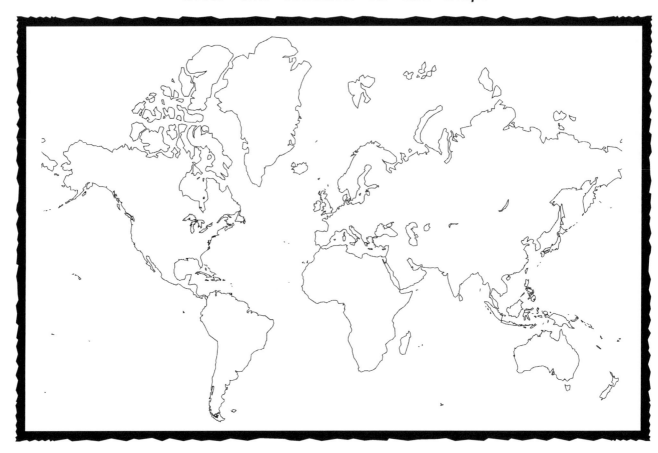

How far do you have to travel to reach this destination?
How would you get there?
What is the cost of travel to this location?
What is the currency called?
What is the current exchange rate?
What language is spoken there?
What is the weather like right now in this location?
What would you pack for this trip?

WRITE, DRAW OR PASTE A PHOTO

Flag	Popular Food
Current Events	Famous Landmark
A Famous Person	A Postage Stamp

WRITE A SHORT STORY, SONG, OR POEM
USING THESE WORDS:

Faith   Fox   Fiddle
Fiji   Fashionable   Fascinate

Title: _____   Date: _____

_____

_____

_____

_____

_____

_____

_____

_____

_____

_____

_____

_____

_____

illustrate your story, song, or poem here

FROM YOUR RESEARCH,
FIND & DEFINE 10 NEW SPELLING WORDS

1. fashionable _____
_____

2. fascinate _____
_____

3. _____
_____

4. _____
_____

5. _____
_____

6. _____
_____

7. _____
_____

8. _____
_____

9. _____
_____

10. _____
_____

CURSIVE PRACTICE

Copy the words on this page.
Use the next page to write
your spelling words in cursive.

Faith

fashionable

fox

plays

the

fiddle

in

Fiji

Cursive Practice

A B C D E F G
H I J K L M
N O P Q R S T
U V W X Y Z

a b c d e f g h
i j k l m n o p
q r s t u v w x
y z 1 2 3 4 5 6 7 8 9 0

GWENEVERE THE GREGARIOUS GIRAFFE PLAYS THE GUITAR IN GAMBIA

MEET THE GIRAFFE

Where do I live?

_____

_____

What do I eat?

_____

_____

_____

My scientific name:

_____

Describe my home/habitat and behavior.

_____

_____

_____

_____

_____

_____

_____

_____

Write about my history or folklore.

_____

_____

_____

_____

_____

ALL ABOUT THE GUITAR

Describe this instrument.

_____

_____

_____

_____

_____

_____

Meaning of its name:

_____

_____

When, where, and by whom was it invented?

_____

_____

_____

_____

How do you play this instrument?

_____

_____

_____

Who is famous for playing this instrument?

_____

_____

_____

_____

GAMBIA

Color this location on the map:

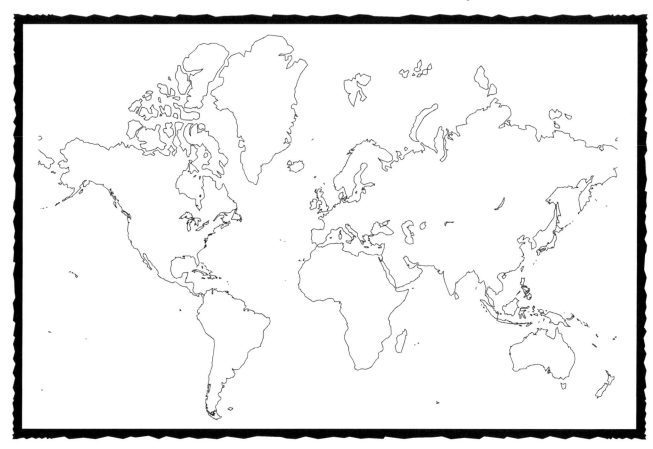

How far do you have to travel to reach this destination?
How would you get there?
What is the cost of travel to this location?
What is the currency called?
What is the current exchange rate?
What language is spoken there?
What is the weather like right now in this location?
What would you pack for this trip?

WRITE, DRAW OR PASTE A PHOTO

Flag	Popular Food

Current Events	Famous Landmark

A Famous Person	A Postage Stamp

TRY A TRADITIONAL RECIPE

Ingredients:

_____

_____

_____

_____

_____

_____

_____

_____

_____

_____

_____

_____

_____

_____

_____

_____

_____

_____

_____

Prep Time:

Oven Temp:

Cook Time:

Directions:

_____

_____

_____

_____

_____

_____

_____

_____

_____

_____

_____

_____

_____

_____

_____

_____

Draw a picture or paste a photo of your culinary masterpiece here

FROM YOUR RESEARCH,
FIND & DEFINE 10 NEW SPELLING WORDS

1. gregarious_____

_____

2. generate_____

_____

3._____

_____

4._____

_____

5._____

_____

6._____

_____

7._____

_____

8._____

_____

9._____

_____

10._____

_____

CURSIVE PRACTICE

Copy the words on this page.
Use the next page to write
your spelling words in cursive.

Gwenevere

gregarious

giraffe

plays

the

guitar

in

Gambia

WORD SEARCH FUN!

```
D H H H E M P A T H E T I C B Y E E A D O G K
R L C N E M A D A P X X B E N J A M I N F F B
U L O N V Y J K V C E M O S E W A Q R X A Q Z
J V U H A A X R A E B C J F J C E S O F A E C
V A R C X A W F R D W L O I L A L K F G R T O
H C A U J I L E A E I D E J E Y B H L Z D S W
N C G E F L B T R N E A F I R Q A X O F V U B
X O E P I A R H Z M E U F M U W N E O C A O E
F R O H D R A I E A L N A S H G O P N R R I L
A D U X D T Z O C R E T R Z R J I Y L O K C L
I I S G L S I P G K P L I Y E C H Z E A V A C
T O M Q E U L I G F H E G W F A S K I T G D B
H N P D O A Q A B U A S W H Y S A W N I Y O N
P J R B F B Z C H F N S S Z M E F H A A A B R
C A T E B M E J D D T O W L Z Y Q O D H G B S
J B A N J O M Y S N K N G R E G A R I O U S W
```

Find the following words in the puzzle.
Words are hidden ↑ ↓ → ← and ↘ .

AARDVARK	BODACIOUS	DAUNTLESS	EZRA
ACCORDION	BRAZIL	DENMARK	FAITH
ADAM	CASEY	DJEMBE	FASHIONABLE
AUSTRALIA	CAT	DOG	FIDDLE
AWESOME	COURAGEOUS	ELEPHANT	FIJI
BANJO	COWBELL	EMPATHETIC	FOX
BEAR	CROATIA	ERHU	GIRAFFE
BENJAMIN	DANIEL	ETHIOPIA	GREGARIOUS

HARMONIE THE HAPPY HAMSTER PLAYS THE HARMONICA IN HUNGARY

MEET THE HAMSTER

Where do I live?

_____

_____

What do I eat?

_____

_____

_____

My scientific name:

_____

Describe my home/habitat and behavior.

_____

_____

_____

_____

_____

_____

_____

Write about my history or folklore.

_____

_____

_____

_____

_____

ALL ABOUT THE HARMONICA

Describe this instrument.

_____
_____
_____
_____
_____
_____

Meaning of its name:

_____
_____

When, where, and by whom was it invented?

_____
_____
_____
_____

How do you play this instrument?

_____
_____
_____
_____

Who is famous for playing this instrument?

_____
_____
_____
_____

HUNGARY

Color this location on the map:

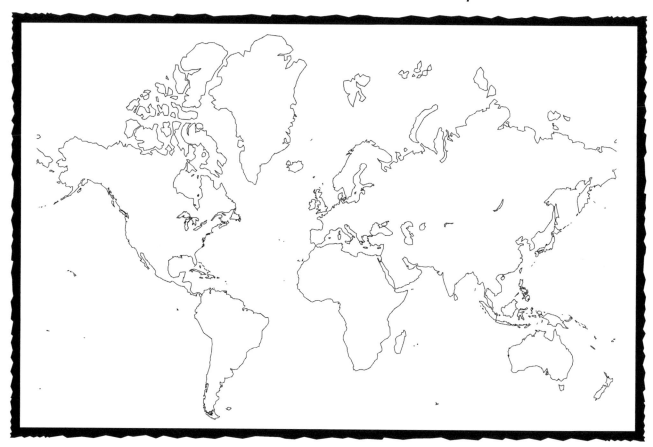

How far do you have to travel to reach this destination?
How would you get there?
What is the cost of travel to this location?
What is the currency called?
What is the current exchange rate?
What language is spoken there?
What is the weather like right now in this location?
What would you pack for this trip?

WRITE, DRAW OR PASTE A PHOTO

Flag	Popular Food

Current Events	Famous Landmark

A Famous Person	A Postage Stamp

DRAW OR PASTE PHOTOS OF TRADITIONAL CLOTHING

FROM YOUR RESEARCH, FIND & DEFINE 10 NEW SPELLING WORDS

1. happy_____

_____

2. harmonize_____

_____

3._____

_____

4._____

_____

5._____

_____

6._____

_____

7._____

_____

8._____

_____

9._____

_____

10._____

_____

CURSIVE PRACTICE
Copy the words on this page.
Use the next page to write
your spelling words in cursive.

Harmonie

happy

hamster

plays

the

harmonica

in

Hungary

84

WRITE A SHORT STORY, SONG, OR POEM
USING THESE WORDS:

Harmonie Hamster Harmonica
Hungary Happy Harmonize

Title: _____   Date: _____

_____

_____

_____

_____

_____

_____

_____

_____

_____

_____

_____

Illustrate your story, song, or poem here

IVAN THE IDEALISTIC IGUANA PLAYS THE INCI IN INDIA

MEET THE IGUANA

Where do I live?

_____

_____

What do I eat?

_____

_____

_____

My scientific name:

_____

Describe my home/habitat and behavior.

_____

_____

_____

_____

_____

_____

_____

Write about my history or folklore.

_____

_____

_____

_____

_____

_____

ALL ABOUT THE INCI

Describe this instrument.

_____

_____

_____

_____

_____

_____

_____

Meaning of its name:

_____

When, where, and by whom was it invented?

_____

_____

_____

_____

How do you play this instrument?

_____

_____

_____

_____

Who is famous for playing this instrument?

_____

_____

_____

_____

_____

INDIA

Color this location on the map:

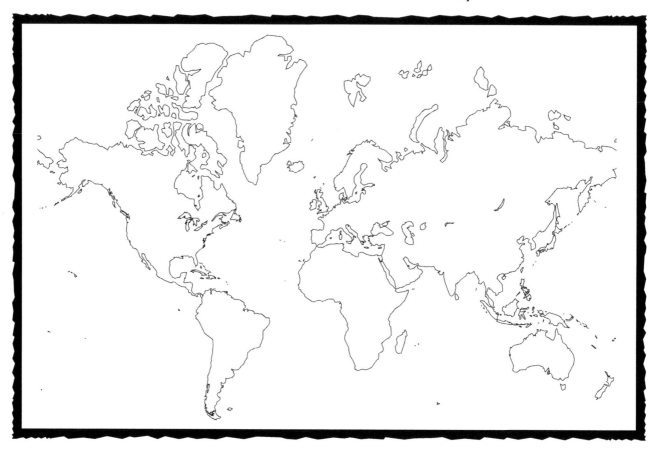

How far do you have to travel to reach this destination?
How would you get there?
What is the cost of travel to this location?
What is the currency called?
What is the current exchange rate?
What language is spoken there?
What is the weather like right now in this location?
What would you pack for this trip?

WRITE, DRAW OR PASTE A PHOTO

Flag	Popular Food
Current Events	Famous Landmark
A Famous Person	A Postage Stamp

FILM STUDY

Find a video about the animal, instrument, or place. Draw something from the video and share what you learned in the space provided below.

Name of Video: _____

Notes:

_____

_____

_____

_____

_____

_____

_____

_____

_____

FROM YOUR RESEARCH,
FIND & DEFINE 10 NEW SPELLING WORDS

1. idealistic_____

_____

2. illuminate_____

_____

3._____

_____

4._____

_____

5._____

_____

6._____

_____

7._____

_____

8._____

_____

9._____

_____

10._____

_____

CURSIVE PRACTICE

Copy the words on this page.
Use the next page to write
your spelling words in cursive.

Ivan

idealistic

iguana

plays

the

inci

in

India

Cursive Practice

A B C D E F G
H I J K L M
N O P Q R S T
U V W X Y Z

a b c d e f g h
i j k l m n o p
q r s t u v w x
y z 1 2 3 4 5 6 7 8 9 0

JAMES THE JOVIAL JAGUAR PLAYS THE JUG IN JAMAICA

MEET THE JAGUAR

Where do I live?

_____

_____

What do I eat?

_____

_____

_____

My scientific name:

_____

Describe my home/habitat and behavior.

_____

_____

_____

_____

_____

_____

_____

Write about my history or folklore.

_____

_____

_____

_____

_____

ALL ABOUT THE JUG

Describe this instrument.

_____
_____
_____
_____
_____
_____
_____

Meaning of its name:

_____
_____

When, where, and by whom was it invented?

_____
_____
_____
_____

How do you play this instrument?

_____
_____
_____
_____

Who is famous for playing this instrument?

_____
_____
_____
_____

JAMAICA

Color this location on the map:

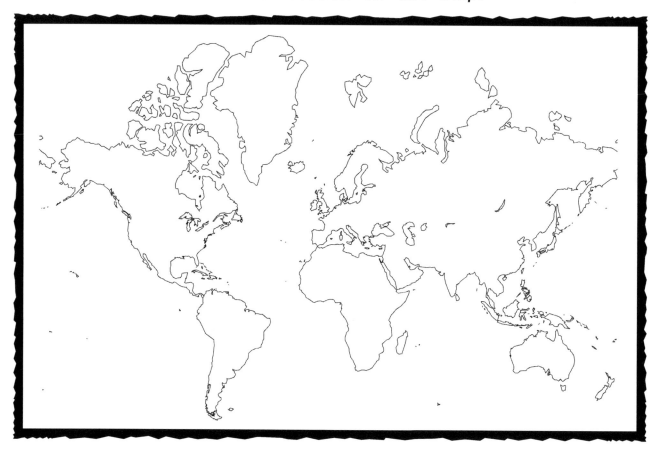

How far do you have to travel to reach this destination?
How would you get there?
What is the cost of travel to this location?
What is the currency called?
What is the current exchange rate?
What language is spoken there?
What is the weather like right now in this location?
What would you pack for this trip?

WRITE, DRAW OR PASTE A PHOTO

Flag	Popular Food
Current Events	**Famous Landmark**
A Famous Person	**A Postage Stamp**

TRY A TRADITIONAL RECIPE

Ingredients:

_____
_____
_____
_____
_____
_____
_____
_____
_____
_____
_____
_____
_____
_____
_____
_____

Prep Time:

Oven Temp:

Cook Time:

Directions:

_____
_____
_____
_____
_____
_____
_____
_____
_____
_____
_____
_____

Draw a picture or paste a photo of your culinary mas-terpiece here

_____
_____
_____
_____

FROM YOUR RESEARCH,
FIND & DEFINE 10 NEW SPELLING WORDS

1. jovial _____

_____

2. journey _____

_____

3. _____

_____

4. _____

_____

5. _____

_____

6. _____

_____

7. _____

_____

8. _____

_____

9. _____

_____

10. _____

_____

CURSIVE PRACTICE
Copy the words on this page.
Use the next page to write
your spelling words in cursive.

James

jovial

jaguar

plays

the

jug

in

Jamacia

WRITE A SHORT STORY, SONG, OR POEM USING THESE WORDS:

James Jaguar Jug
Jamaica Jovial Journey

Title: _____   Date: _____

_____

_____

_____

_____

_____

_____

_____

_____

_____

_____

_____

_____

Illustrate your story, song, or poem here

KAILANI THE KIND KANGAROO PLAYS THE KAZOO IN KAZAKHSTAN

MEET THE KANGAROO

Where do I live?

_____

_____

What do I eat?

_____

_____

_____

My scientific name:

_____

Describe my home/habitat and behavior.

_____

_____

_____

_____

_____

_____

_____

Write about my history or folklore.

_____

_____

_____

_____

_____

ALL ABOUT THE KAZOO

Describe this instrument.

_____

_____

_____

_____

_____

_____

_____

Meaning of its name:

_____

_____

When, where, and by whom was it invented?

_____

_____

_____

_____

_____

How do you play this instrument?

_____

_____

_____

_____

Who is famous for playing this instrument?

_____

_____

_____

_____

KAZAKHSTAN

Color this location on the map:

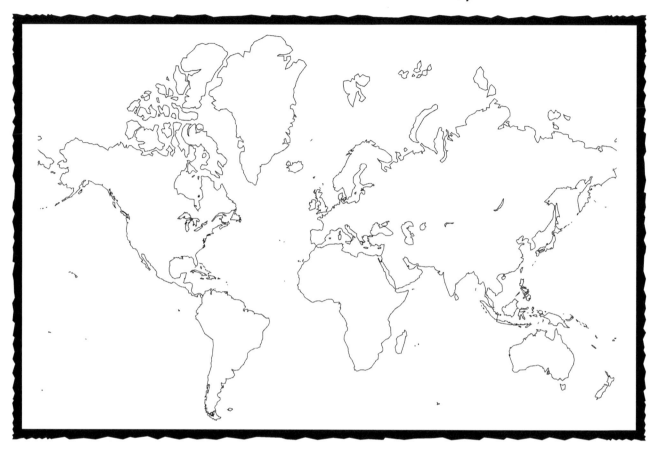

How far do you have to travel to reach this destination?
How would you get there?
What is the cost of travel to this location?
What is the currency called?
What is the current exchange rate?
What language is spoken there?
What is the weather like right now in this location?
What would you pack for this trip?

WRITE, DRAW OR PASTE A PHOTO

Flag	Popular Food
Current Events	Famous Landmark
A Famous Person	A Postage Stamp

DRAW OR PASTE PHOTOS OF TRADITIONAL CLOTHING

FROM YOUR RESEARCH,
FIND & DEFINE 10 NEW SPELLING WORDS

1. kind _____

_____

2. kindle _____

_____

3. _____

_____

4. _____

_____

5. _____

_____

6. _____

_____

7. _____

_____

8. _____

_____

9. _____

_____

10. _____

_____

CURSIVE PRACTICE

Copy the words on this page.
Use the next page to write
your spelling words in cursive.

Kaitani

kind

kangaroo

plays

the

kazoo

in

Kazakhstan

TRY A TRADITIONAL RECIPE

Ingredients:

_____
_____
_____
_____
_____
_____
_____
_____
_____
_____
_____
_____
_____
_____
_____
_____
_____
_____
_____

Prep Time:

Oven Temp:

Cook Time:

Directions:

_____
_____
_____
_____
_____
_____
_____
_____
_____
_____
_____
_____
_____
_____
_____
_____

Draw a picture or paste a photo of your culinary masterpiece here

LINCOLN THE LAWFUL LION PLAYS THE LUTE IN LITHUANIA

MEET THE LION

My scientific name:

_____

Where do I live?

_____

_____

What do I eat?

_____

_____

_____

Describe my home/habitat and behavior.

_____

_____

_____

_____

_____

_____

_____

Write about my history or folklore.

_____

_____

_____

_____

_____

ALL ABOUT THE LUTE

Describe this instrument.

_____
_____
_____
_____
_____
_____

Meaning of its name:

_____
_____

When, where, and by whom was it invented?

_____
_____
_____
_____

How do you play this instrument?

_____
_____
_____

Who is famous for playing this instrument?

_____
_____
_____
_____

LITHUANIA

Color this location on the map:

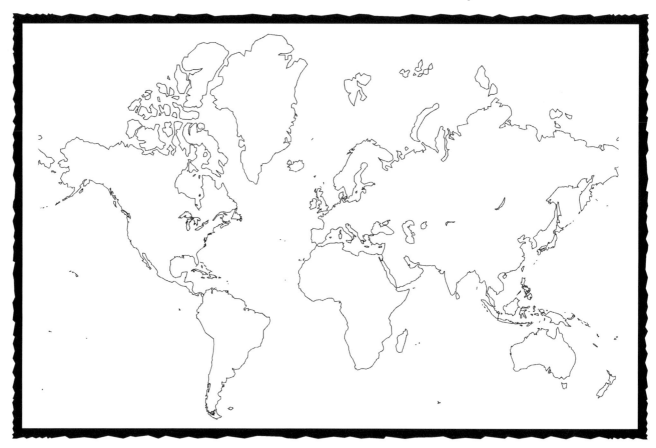

How far do you have to travel to reach this destination?
How would you get there?
What is the cost of travel to this location?
What is the currency called?
What is the current exchange rate?
What language is spoken there?
What is the weather like right now in this location?
What would you pack for this trip?

WRITE, DRAW OR PASTE A PHOTO

Flag	Popular Food
Current Events	**Famous Landmark**
A Famous Person	A Postage Stamp

CURSIVE PRACTICE

Copy the words on this page.
Use the next page to write
your spelling words in cursive.

Lincoln

lawful

lion

plays

the

lute

in

Lithuania

WRITE A SHORT STORY, SONG, OR POEM USING THESE WORDS:

Lincoln Lion Lute
Lithuania Lawful Launch

Title: _____ Date: _____

_____

_____

_____

_____

_____

_____

_____

_____

_____

_____

_____

_____

Illustrate your story, song, or poem here

MIGUEL THE MELLOW MONKEY PLAYS THE MANDOLIN IN MOROCCO

MEET THE MONKEY

Where do I live?

_____

_____

What do I eat?

_____

_____

_____

My scientific name:

_____

Describe my home/habitat and behavior.

_____

_____

_____

_____

_____

_____

_____

_____

Write about my history or folklore.

_____

_____

_____

_____

_____

ALL ABOUT THE MANDOLIN

Describe this instrument.

_____

_____

_____

_____

_____

_____

Meaning of its name:

_____

_____

When, where, and by whom was it invented?

_____

_____

_____

_____

How do you play this instrument?

_____

_____

_____

Who is famous for playing this instrument?

_____

_____

_____

_____

MOROCCO

Color this location on the map:

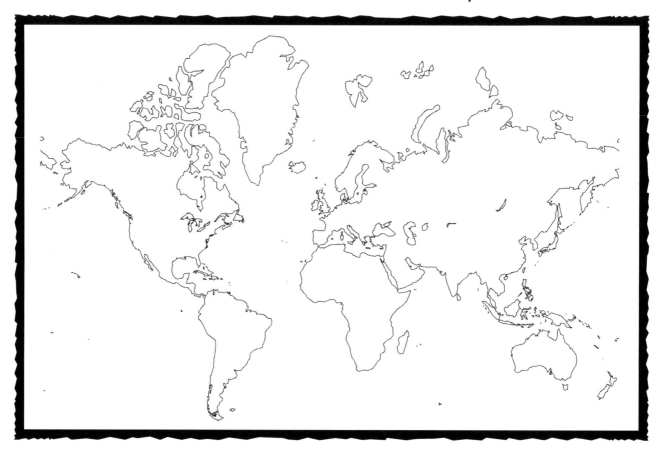

How far do you have to travel to reach this destination?
How would you get there?
What is the cost of travel to this location?
What is the currency called?
What is the current exchange rate?
What language is spoken there?
What is the weather like right now in this location?
What would you pack for this trip?

WRITE, DRAW OR PASTE A PHOTO

Flag	Popular Food

Current Events	Famous Landmark

A Famous Person	A Postage Stamp

TRY A TRADITIONAL RECIPE

Ingredients:

_____

_____

_____

_____

_____

_____

_____

_____

_____

_____

_____

_____

_____

_____

_____

_____

_____

_____

_____

Prep Time:

Oven Temp:

Cook Time:

Directions:

_____

_____

_____

_____

_____

_____

_____

_____

_____

_____

_____

_____

_____

_____

Draw a picture or paste a photo of your culinary masterpiece here

_____

_____

_____

_____

_____

_____

_____

FROM YOUR RESEARCH,
FIND & DEFINE 10 NEW SPELLING WORDS

1. mellow_____

_____

2. measure_____

_____

3._____

_____

4._____

_____

5._____

_____

6._____

_____

7._____

_____

8._____

_____

9._____

_____

10._____

_____

CURSIVE PRACTICE

Copy the words on this page.
Use the next page to write
your spelling words in cursive.

Miguel

mellow

monkey

plays

the

mandolin

in

Morocco

WORD SEARCH FUN!

```
I U N L O C N I L L H J O V I A L F W G Q S M
O G U J L Z J V V L A G V I L F C B A K W X H
C B Z Q U D A E K L R V F F N I Q S N A L J U
R K M K F H M R F E M Q W K I D O L A N J V N
H V J Y W O A E I U O A U F A V I N U G B M G
A B S M A W I V M G N T G U Q Z A A G A C E A
R Q Y N L J C E O I I M J U I Q A N I R R L R
M Y P I U A A N N M E I A J I L J K J O Y L Y
O Z P L V M W E K P N N G N G T R C H O B O Y
N L A U Y E C W E M K A U J D K A B Z S Q W S
I G H T L S N G Y E F L A C H O S R N M T Y B
C N I E D N I K L O Z I R A K E L S Q Y E A B
A L Q L R E T S M A H A Q L K Q T I B N B Y N
F A Q U O Y K A Z O O K V T W J D G N G R J T
D F Z H J S X L D F P I D E A L I S T I C Z Q
L I T H U A N I A I N C I A I B M A G W P B E
```

Find the following words in the puzzle.
Words are hidden ↑ ↓ → ← and ↘ .

GAMBIA	IDEALISTIC	JOVIAL	LINCOLN
GUITAR	IGUANA	JUG	LION
GWENEVERE	INCI	KAILANI	LITHUANIA
HAMSTER	INDIA	KANGAROO	LUTE
HAPPY	IVAN	KAZAKHSTAN	MANDOLIN
HARMONICA	JAGUAR	KAZOO	MELLOW
HARMONIE	JAMAICA	KIND	MIGUEL
HUNGARY	JAMES	LAWFUL	MONKEY

NOAH THE NIMBLE NUTRIA PLAYS THE NEY IN NORWAY

MEET THE NUTRIA

Where do I live?

_____

_____

What do I eat?

_____

_____

_____

My scientific name:

_____

Describe my home/habitat and behavior.

_____

_____

_____

_____

_____

_____

_____

_____

Write about my history or folklore.

_____

_____

_____

_____

_____

ALL ABOUT THE NEY

Describe this instrument.

_____

_____

_____

_____

_____

_____

_____

Meaning of its name:

_____

_____

When, where, and by whom was it invented?

_____

_____

_____

_____

How do you play this instrument?

_____

_____

_____

_____

Who is famous for playing this instrument?

_____

_____

_____

_____

NORWAY

Color this location on the map:

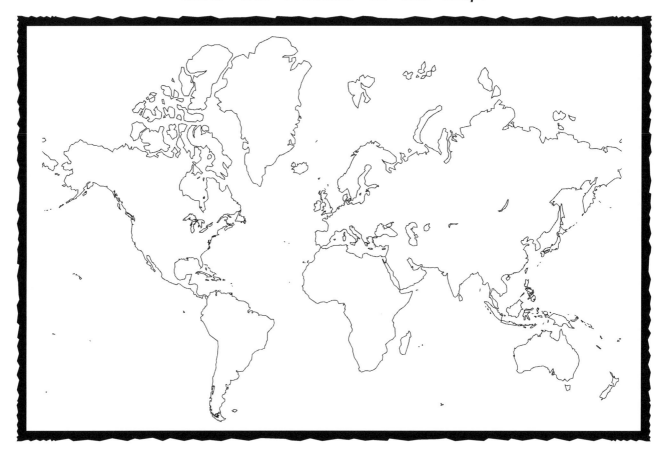

How far do you have to travel to reach this destination?
How would you get there?
What is the cost of travel to this location?
What is the currency called?
What is the current exchange rate?
What language is spoken there?
What is the weather like right now in this location?
What would you pack for this trip?

WRITE, DRAW OR PASTE A PHOTO

Flag	Popular Food
Current Events	Famous Landmark
A Famous Person	A Postage Stamp

DRAW OR PASTE PHOTOS OF TRADITIONAL CLOTHING

FROM YOUR RESEARCH,
FIND & DEFINE 10 NEW SPELLING WORDS

1. nimble_____

_____

2. negotiate_____

_____

3. _____

_____

4. _____

_____

5. _____

_____

6. _____

_____

7. _____

_____

8. _____

_____

9. _____

_____

10. _____

_____

CURSIVE PRACTICE
Copy the words on this page.
Use the next page to write
your spelling words in cursive.

Noah

nimble

nutria

plays

the

ney

in

Norway

142

WRITE A SHORT STORY, SONG, OR POEM
USING THESE WORDS:
Noah Nutria Ney
Norway Nimble Negotiate

Title: _____   Date: _____

_____

_____

_____

_____

_____

_____

_____

_____

_____

_____

_____

_____

Illustrate your story, song, or poem here

OLIVER THE OBLIGING OPOSSUM PLAYS THE OBOE IN ODESSA

MEET THE OPOSSUM

Where do I live?

_____

_____

What do I eat?

_____

_____

_____

My scientific name:

_____

Describe my home/habitat and behavior.

_____

_____

_____

_____

_____

_____

_____

Write about my history or folklore.

_____

_____

_____

_____

_____

ALL ABOUT THE OBOE

Describe this instrument.

_____

_____

_____

_____

_____

_____

Meaning of its name:

_____

_____

When, where, and by whom was it invented?

_____

_____

_____

_____

How do you play this instrument?

_____

_____

_____

Who is famous for playing this instrument?

_____

_____

_____

_____

ODESSA

Color this location on the map:

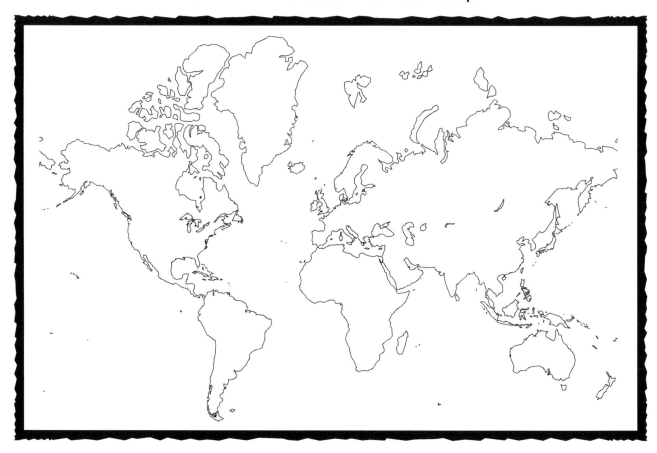

How far do you have to travel to reach this destination?
How would you get there?
What is the cost of travel to this location?
What is the currency called?
What is the current exchange rate?
What language is spoken there?
What is the weather like right now in this location?
What would you pack for this trip?

WRITE, DRAW OR PASTE A PHOTO

Flag	Popular Food
Current Events	**Famous Landmark**
A Famous Person	**A Postage Stamp**

TRY A TRADITIONAL RECIPE

Ingredients:

_____

Directions:

_____

_____

Prep Time:

Oven Temp:

Cook Time:

Draw a picture or paste a photo of your culinary masterpiece here

FROM YOUR RESEARCH,
FIND & DEFINE 10 NEW SPELLING WORDS

1. obliging_____

_____

2. originate_____

_____

3._____

_____

4._____

_____

5._____

_____

6._____

_____

7._____

_____

8._____

_____

9._____

_____

10._____

_____

CURSIVE PRACTICE
Copy the words on this page.
Use the next page to write
your spelling words in cursive.

Oliver

obliging

opossum

plays

the

oboe

in

FILM STUDY

Find a video about the animal, instrument, or place. Draw something from the video and share what you learned in the space provided below.

Name of Video: _____

Notes:

_____

_____

_____

_____

_____

_____

_____

_____

PETER THE PEACEFUL PANDA PLAYS
THE PAN PIPES IN PERU

MEET THE PANDA

My scientific name:

_____

Where do I live?

_____

_____

What do I eat?

_____

_____

_____

Describe my home/habitat and behavior.

_____

_____

_____

_____

_____

_____

_____

Write about my history or folklore.

_____

_____

_____

_____

_____

ALL ABOUT THE PAN PIPES

Describe this instrument.

_____

_____

_____

_____

_____

_____

Meaning of its name:

_____

_____

When, where, and by whom was it invented?

_____

_____

_____

_____

How do you play this instrument?

_____

_____

_____

Who is famous for playing this instrument?

_____

_____

_____

_____

PERU

Color this location on the map:

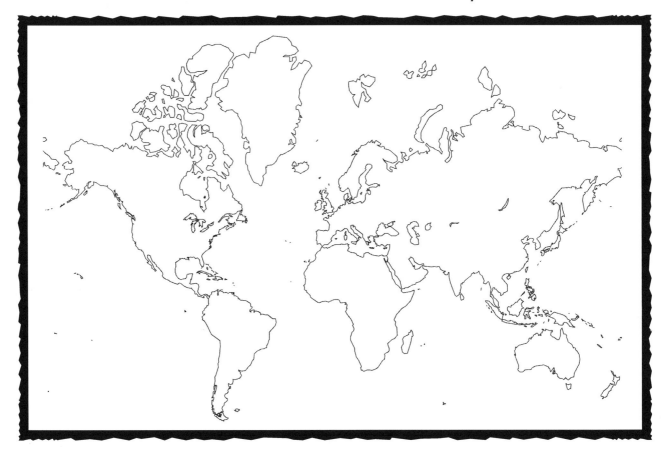

How far do you have to travel to reach this destination?
How would you get there?
What is the cost of travel to this location?
What is the currency called?
What is the current exchange rate?
What language is spoken there?
What is the weather like right now in this location?
What would you pack for this trip?

WRITE, DRAW OR PASTE A PHOTO

Flag	Popular Food

Current Events	Famous Landmark

A Famous Person	A Postage Stamp

DRAW OR PASTE PHOTOS OF TRADITIONAL CLOTHING

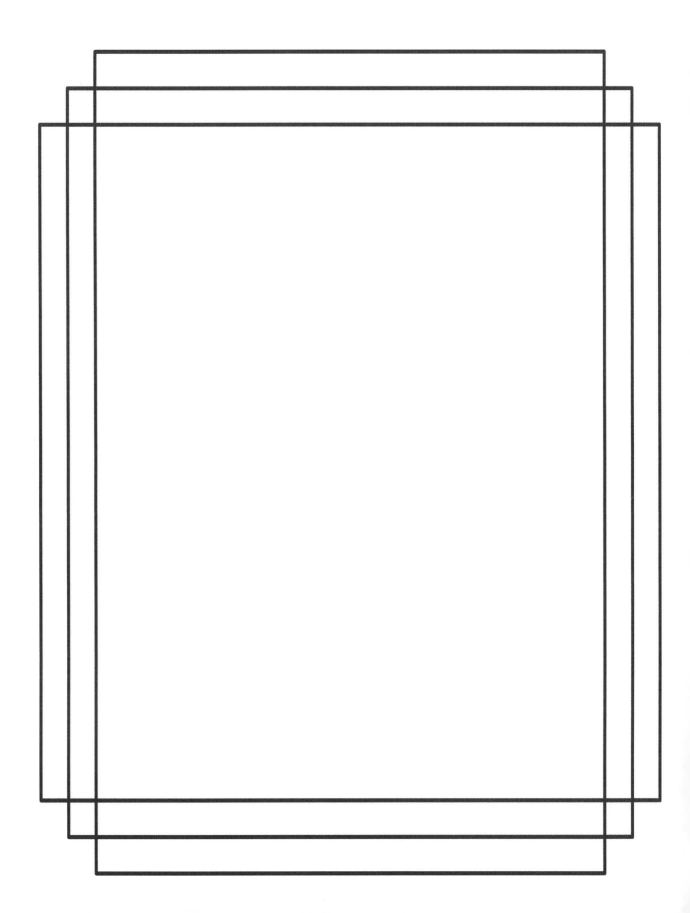

FROM YOUR RESEARCH,
FIND & DEFINE 10 NEW SPELLING WORDS

1. peaceful_____

_____

2. postulate_____

_____

3. _____

_____

4. _____

_____

5. _____

_____

6. _____

_____

7. _____

_____

8. _____

_____

9. _____

_____

10. _____

_____

CURSIVE PRACTICE

Copy the words on this page. Use the next page to write your spelling words in cursive.

Peter

peaceful

panda

plays

the

pan pipes

in

Peru

Cursive Practice

A B C D E F G
H I J K L M
N O P Q R S T
U V W X Y Z

a b c d e f g h
i j k l m n o p
q r s t u v w x
y z 1 2 3 4 5 6 7 8 9 0

QUIANA THE QUIZZICAL QUOKKA PLAYS THE QUENA IN QUEBEC CITY

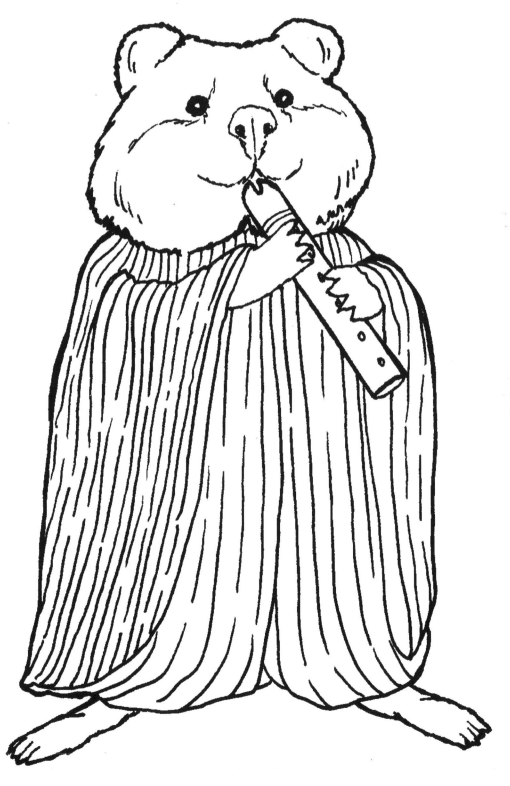

MEET THE QUOKKA

Where do I live?

_____

_____

What do I eat?

_____

_____

My scientific name:

_____

Describe my home/habitat and behavior.

_____

_____

_____

_____

_____

_____

_____

Write about my history or folklore.

_____

_____

_____

_____

_____

ALL ABOUT THE QATAR

Describe this instrument.

_____

_____

_____

_____

_____

_____

Meaning of its name:

_____

_____

When, where, and by whom was it invented?

_____

_____

_____

_____

How do you play this instrument?

_____

_____

_____

Who is famous for playing this instrument?

_____

_____

_____

_____

QUEBEC CITY

Color this location on the map:

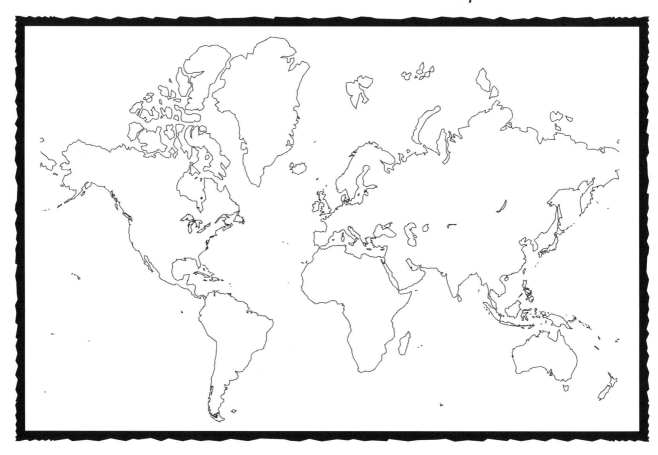

| How far do you have to travel to reach this destination? |
| How would you get there? |
| What is the cost of travel to this location? |
| What is the currency called? |
| What is the current exchange rate? |
| What language is spoken there? |
| What is the weather like right now in this location? |
| What would you pack for this trip? |

WRITE, DRAW OR PASTE A PHOTO

Flag	Popular Food

Current Events	Famous Landmark

A Famous Person	A Postage Stamp

WRITE A SHORT STORY, SONG, OR POEM USING THESE WORDS:

Quiana Quokka Quena
Quebec City Quizzical Qualify

Title: _____   Date: _____

_____

_____

_____

_____

_____

_____

_____

_____

_____

_____

_____

_____

Illustrate your story, song, or poem here

FROM YOUR RESEARCH, FIND & DEFINE 10 NEW SPELLING WORDS

1. quizzical _____

_____

2. qualify _____

_____

3. _____

_____

4. _____

_____

5. _____

_____

6. _____

_____

7. _____

_____

8. _____

_____

9. _____

_____

10. _____

_____

CURSIVE PRACTICE
Copy the words on this page.
Use the next page to write
your spelling words in cursive.

Quiana

quizzical

quokka

plays

the

quena

in

Quebec City

FILM STUDY

Find a video about the animal, instrument, or place.
Draw something from the video and share what you learned
in the space provided below.

Name of Video: _____

Notes:

_____
_____
_____
_____
_____
_____
_____
_____

RUBEN THE ROVING RACCOON
PLAYS THE RECORDER IN RWANDA

MEET THE RACCOON

Where do I live?

_____

_____

What do I eat?

My scientific name:

_____

_____

_____

_____

Describe my home/habitat and behavior.

_____

_____

_____

_____

_____

_____

_____

Write about my history or folklore.

_____

_____

_____

_____

_____

ALL ABOUT THE RECORDER

Describe this instrument.

_____
_____
_____
_____
_____
_____

Meaning of its name:

_____
_____

When, where, and by whom was it invented?

_____
_____
_____
_____

How do you play this instrument?

_____
_____
_____

Who is famous for playing this instrument?

_____
_____
_____
_____

RWANDA

Color this location on the map:

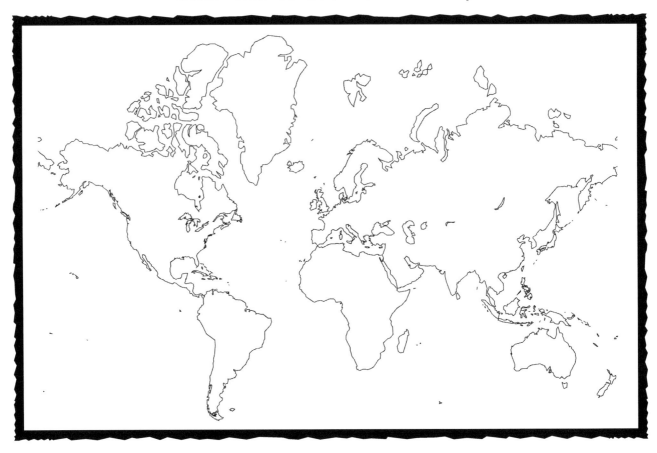

How far do you have to travel to reach this destination?
How would you get there?
What is the cost of travel to this location?
What is the currency called?
What is the current exchange rate?
What language is spoken there?
What is the weather like right now in this location?
What would you pack for this trip?

WRITE, DRAW OR PASTE A PHOTO

Flag	Popular Food

Current Events	Famous Landmark

A Famous Person	A Postage Stamp

DRAW OR PASTE PHOTOS OF TRADITIONAL CLOTHING

FROM YOUR RESEARCH,
FIND & DEFINE 10 NEW SPELLING WORDS

1. roving _____

_____

2. recommend _____

_____

3. _____

_____

4. _____

_____

5. _____

_____

6. _____

_____

7. _____

_____

8. _____

_____

9. _____

_____

10. _____

_____

CURSIVE PRACTICE

Copy the words on this page.
Use the next page to write
your spelling words in cursive.

Ruben

roving

raccoon

plays

the

recorder

in

Rwanda

TRY A TRADITIONAL RECIPE

Ingredients:

_____
_____
_____
_____
_____
_____
_____
_____
_____
_____
_____
_____
_____
_____
_____
_____
_____
_____
_____
_____

Prep Time:

Oven Temp:

Cook Time:

Directions:

_____
_____
_____
_____
_____
_____
_____
_____
_____
_____
_____
_____
_____
_____
_____
_____
_____
_____

Draw a picture or paste a photo of your culinary masterpiece here

SERGIO THE SENSITIVE SKUNK PLAYS THE SAXOPHONE IN SPAIN

MEET THE SKUNK

Where do I live?

_____

_____

What do I eat?

My scientific name:

_____

_____

_____

_____

Describe my home/habitat and behavior.

_____

_____

_____

_____

_____

_____

_____

Write about my history or folklore.

_____

_____

_____

_____

_____

ALL ABOUT THE SAXOPHONE

Describe this instrument.

_____

_____

_____

_____

_____

_____

Meaning of its name:

_____

_____

When, where, and by whom was it invented?

_____

_____

_____

_____

How do you play this instrument?

_____

_____

_____

Who is famous for playing this instrument?

_____

_____

_____

_____

SPAIN

Color this location on the map:

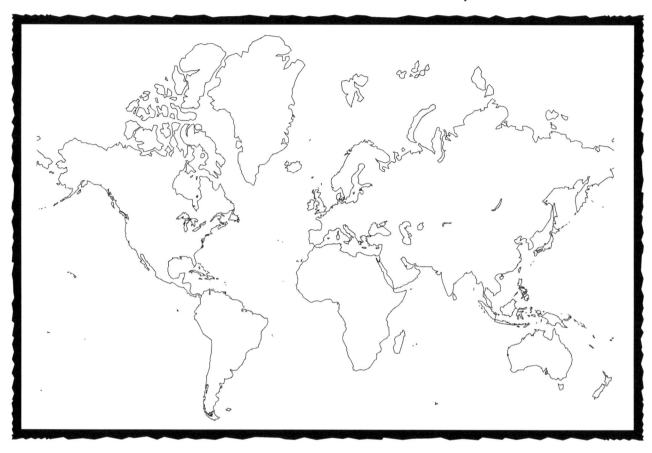

How far do you have to travel to reach this destination?
How would you get there?
What is the cost of travel to this location?
What is the currency called?
What is the current exchange rate?
What language is spoken there?
What is the weather like right now in this location?
What would you pack for this trip?

WRITE, DRAW OR PASTE A PHOTO

Flag	Popular Food
Current Events	**Famous Landmark**
A Famous Person	**A Postage Stamp**

WRITE A SHORT STORY, SONG, OR POEM USING THESE WORDS:

Sergio Skunk Saxophone
Spain Sensitive Sentimentalize

Title: _____   Date: _____

_____

_____

_____

_____

_____

_____

_____

_____

_____

_____

_____

_____

Illustrate your story, song, or poem here

FROM YOUR RESEARCH,
FIND & DEFINE IO NEW SPELLING WORDS

1. sensitive_____

_____

2. sentimentalize_____

_____

3._____

_____

4._____

_____

5._____

_____

6._____

_____

7._____

_____

8._____

_____

9._____

_____

10._____

_____

CURSIVE PRACTICE

Copy the words on this page.
Use the next page to write
your spelling words in cursive.

Sergio

sensitive

skunk

plays

the

saxophone

in

Spain

WORD SEARCH FUN!

```
L  N  O  O  C  C  A  R  W  Z  E  N  N  O  A  H  T  Y  Y  L  B  S  K
G  S  O  Y  N  D  U  R  E  P  J  B  Z  L  I  A  D  U  D  E  Z  N  M
C  F  E  N  O  H  P  O  X  A  S  U  K  U  C  N  Q  S  C  N  D  O  U
S  Q  U  E  N  A  K  R  O  T  P  E  N  F  G  T  N  P  L  J  X  R  S
E  F  C  B  S  R  N  P  P  N  G  D  I  E  N  H  F  B  Y  P  M  W  S
N  W  Q  D  M  E  U  S  R  U  V  J  M  C  I  O  F  T  J  R  B  A  O
S  S  U  O  O  T  K  P  S  O  P  L  B  A  G  U  G  Y  Z  E  N  Y  P
I  P  I  N  R  E  S  A  I  R  V  K  L  E  I  G  O  T  L  V  U  O  O
T  A  Z  D  O  P  H  N  R  R  I  E  P  L  H  O  I  K  I  T  D  K
I  I  Z  Y  C  U  N  P  W  E  Q  F  N  T  B  T  I  C  I  L  R  E  Y
V  N  I  U  C  U  A  I  A  D  D  U  B  G  O  F  G  C  E  O  I  S  A
E  T  C  T  O  O  T  P  N  R  Y  O  O  D  B  U  R  E  N  B  A  A  D
N  V  A  Z  Z  I  G  E  D  O  W  L  B  K  Y  L  E  B  E  V  V  R  N
X  T  L  I  U  M  I  S  A  C  F  O  O  O  K  J  S  E  Y  O  D  W  A
V  E  Q  U  I  A  N  A  S  E  C  R  A  W  E  A  J  U  Y  U  J  B  P
R  U  B  E  N  T  K  B  Y  R  W  T  W  P  R  F  N  Q  P  I  A  N  W
```

Find the following words in the puzzle.
Words are hidden ↑ ↓ → ← and ↘ .

MOROCCO	ODESA	QUEBECCITY	RUBEN
NEY	OLIVER	QUENA	RWANDA
NIMBLE	OPOSSUM	QUIANA	SAXOPHONE
NOAH	PANDA	QUIZZICAL	SENSITIVE
NORWAY	PANPIPES	QUOKKA	SERGIO
NUTRIA	PEACEFUL	RACCOON	SKUNK
OBLIGING	PERU	RECORDER	SPAIN
OBOE	PETER	ROVING	THOUGHTFUL

TALLULAH THE THOUGHTFUL TIGER PLAYS THE TAMBOURINE IN TURKEY

MEET THE TIGER

Where do I live?

_____

_____

What do I eat?

_____

_____

_____

My scientific name:

_____

Describe my home/habitat and behavior.

_____

_____

_____

_____

_____

_____

_____

Write about my history or folklore.

_____

_____

_____

_____

_____

ALL ABOUT THE TAMBOURINE

Describe this instrument.

_____

_____

_____

_____

_____

Meaning of its name:

_____

_____

When, where, and by whom was it invented?

_____

_____

_____

_____

How do you play this instrument?

_____

_____

_____

_____

Who is famous for playing this instrument?

_____

_____

_____

_____

TURKEY

Color this location on the map:

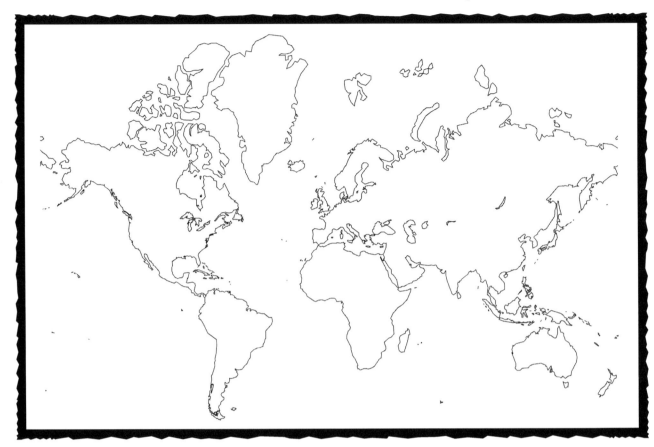

How far do you have to travel to reach this destination?
How would you get there?
What is the cost of travel to this location?
What is the currency called?
What is the current exchange rate?
What language is spoken there?
What is the weather like right now in this location?
What would you pack for this trip?

WRITE, DRAW OR PASTE A PHOTO

Flag	Popular Food

Current Events	Famous Landmark

A Famous Person	A Postage Stamp

DRAW OR PASTE PHOTOS OF TRADITIONAL CLOTHING

FROM YOUR RESEARCH,
FIND & DEFINE 10 NEW SPELLING WORDS

1. thoughtful_____

_____

2. thrive_____

_____

3._____

_____

4._____

_____

5._____

_____

6._____

_____

7._____

_____

8._____

_____

9._____

_____

10._____

_____

CURSIVE PRACTICE

Copy the words on this page.
Use the next page to write
your spelling words in cursive.

Tallulah

thoughtful

tiger

plays

the

tambourine

in

Turkey

FILM STUDY

Find a video about the animal, instrument, or place. Draw something from the video and share what you learned in the space provided below.

Name of Video: _____

Notes:

_____

_____

_____

_____

_____

_____

_____

_____

ULISES THE UNSELFISH UAKARI PLAYS THE UKULELE IN URUGUAY

MEET THE UAKARI

Where do I live?

_____

_____

What do I eat?

My scientific name:

_____

_____

_____

_____

Describe my home/habitat and behavior.

_____

_____

_____

_____

_____

_____

_____

Write about my history or folklore.

_____

_____

_____

_____

_____

ALL ABOUT THE UKULELE

Describe this instrument.

_____

_____

_____

_____

_____

_____

_____

Meaning of its name:

_____

_____

When, where, and by whom was it invented?

_____

_____

_____

_____

How do you play this instrument?

_____

_____

_____

_____

Who is famous for playing this instrument?

_____

_____

_____

_____

URUGUAY

Color this location on the map:

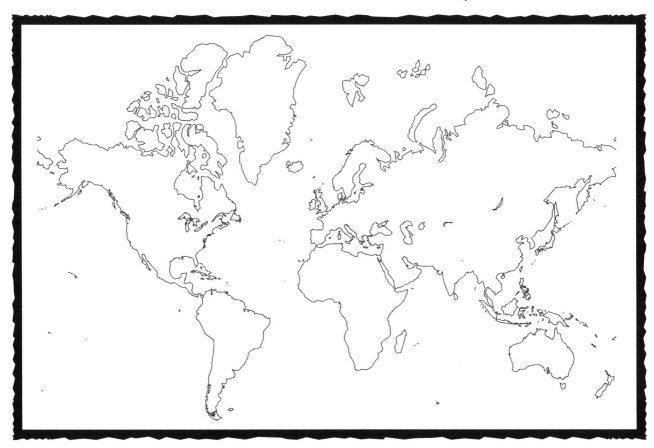

How far do you have to travel to reach this destination?
How would you get there?
What is the cost of travel to this location?
What is the currency called?
What is the current exchange rate?
What language is spoken there?
What is the weather like right now in this location?
What would you pack for this trip?

WRITE, DRAW OR PASTE A PHOTO

Flag	Popular Food
Current Events	**Famous Landmark**
A Famous Person	**A Postage Stamp**

TRY A TRADITIONAL RECIPE

Ingredients:

Directions:

_____

_____

_____

_____

_____

_____

_____

_____

_____

_____

_____

_____

_____

_____

_____

_____

_____

Prep Time:

Oven Temp:

Cook Time:

Draw a picture or paste a photo of your culinary masterpiece here

FROM YOUR RESEARCH,
FIND & DEFINE 10 NEW SPELLING WORDS

1. unselfish_____

_____

2. undergo_____

_____

3._____

_____

4._____

_____

5._____

_____

6._____

_____

7._____

_____

8._____

_____

9._____

_____

10._____

_____

CURSIVE PRACTICE

Copy the words on this page.
Use the next page to write
your spelling words in cursive.

Ulises

unselfish

uakari

plays

the

ukulele

in

Uruguay

WRITE A SHORT STORY, SONG, OR POEM
USING THESE WORDS:

Ulises Uakari Ukulele
Uruguay Unselfish Undergo

Title: _____   Date: _____

_____

_____

_____

_____

_____

_____

_____

_____

_____

_____

_____

_____

Illustrate your story, song, or poem here

VEDA THE VOCIFEROUS VICUNA
PLAYS THE VOLYNKA IN VENEZUELA

MEET THE VICUNA

My scientific name:

_____

Where do I live?

_____

_____

What do I eat?

_____

_____

_____

Describe my home/habitat and behavior.

_____

_____

_____

_____

_____

_____

_____

Write about my history or folklore.

_____

_____

_____

_____

_____

ALL ABOUT THE VOLYNKA

Describe this instrument.

_____

_____

_____

_____

_____

_____

_____

Meaning of its name:

_____

_____

When, where, and by whom was it invented?

_____

_____

_____

_____

How do you play this instrument?

_____

_____

_____

_____

Who is famous for playing this instrument?

_____

_____

_____

_____

VENEZUELA

Color this location on the map:

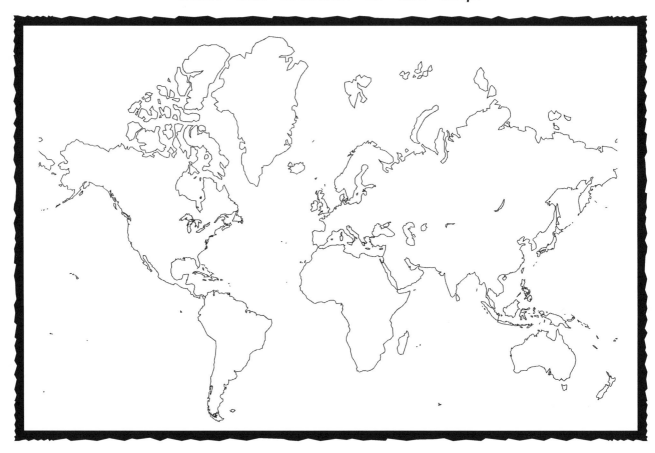

How far do you have to travel to reach this destination?
How would you get there?
What is the cost of travel to this location?
What is the currency called?
What is the current exchange rate?
What language is spoken there?
What is the weather like right now in this location?
What would you pack for this trip?

WRITE, DRAW OR PASTE A PHOTO

Flag	Popular Food

Current Events	Famous Landmark

A Famous Person	A Postage Stamp

FILM STUDY

Find a video about the animal, instrument, or place. Draw something from the video and share what you learned in the space provided below.

Name of Video: _____

Notes:

_____

_____

_____

_____

_____

_____

_____

_____

FROM YOUR RESEARCH,
FIND & DEFINE 10 NEW SPELLING WORDS

1. vociferous _____

_____

2. venerate _____

_____

3. _____

_____

4. _____

_____

5. _____

_____

6. _____

_____

7. _____

_____

8. _____

_____

9. _____

_____

10. _____

_____

CURSIVE PRACTICE
Copy the words on this page.
Use the next page to write
your spelling words in cursive.

Veda

vociferous

vicuna

plays

the

volynka

in

Venezuela

Cursive Practice

A B C D E F G
H I J K L M
N O P Q R S T
U V W X Y Z

a b c d e f g h
i j k l m n o p
q r s t u v w x
y z 1 2 3 4 5 6 7 8 9 0

WILMINA THE WARMHEARTED WOLF PLAYS THE WASHTUB BASS IN WOLFSBURG

MEET THE WOLF

My scientific name:

_____

Where do I live?

_____

_____

What do I eat?

_____

_____

Describe my home/habitat and behavior.

_____

_____

_____

_____

_____

_____

_____

_____

Write about my history or folklore.

_____

_____

_____

_____

_____

_____

ALL ABOUT THE WASHTUB BASS

Describe this instrument.

_____
_____
_____
_____
_____
_____

Meaning of its name:

_____
_____

When, where, and by whom was it invented?

_____
_____
_____
_____

How do you play this instrument?

_____
_____
_____

Who is famous for playing this instrument?

_____
_____
_____
_____

WOLFSBURG

Color this location on the map:

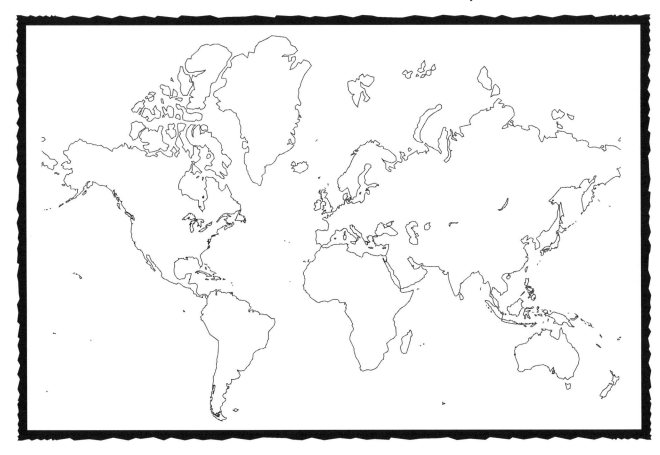

How far do you have to travel to reach this destination?
How would you get there?
What is the cost of travel to this location?
What is the currency called?
What is the current exchange rate?
What language is spoken there?
What is the weather like right now in this location?
What would you pack for this trip?

WRITE, DRAW OR PASTE A PHOTO

Flag	Popular Food

Current Events	Famous Landmark

A Famous Person	A Postage Stamp

DRAW OR PASTE PHOTOS OF TRADITIONAL CLOTHING

FROM YOUR RESEARCH,
FIND & DEFINE 10 NEW SPELLING WORDS

1. warmhearted_____

_____

2. welcome_____

_____

3._____

_____

4._____

_____

5._____

_____

6._____

_____

7._____

_____

8._____

_____

9._____

_____

10._____

_____

WRITE A SHORT STORY, SONG, OR POEM USING THESE WORDS:

Wilmina Wolf Washtub Bass
Wolfsburg Warmhearted Welcome

Title: _____   Date: _____

_____

_____

_____

_____

_____

_____

_____

_____

_____

_____

_____

_____

Illustrate your story, song, or poem here

XANDER THE XENODOCHIAL XERUS
PLAYS THE XYLOPHONE IN XAI-XAI

MEET THE XERUS

My scientific name:

_____

Where do I live?

_____

_____

What do I eat?

_____

_____

_____

Describe my home/habitat and behavior.

_____

_____

_____

_____

_____

_____

_____

_____

Write about my history or folklore.

_____

_____

_____

_____

_____

_____

ALL ABOUT THE XYLOPHONE

Describe this instrument.

_____

_____

_____

_____

_____

_____

Meaning of its name:

_____

_____

When, where, and by whom was it invented?

_____

_____

_____

_____

How do you play this instrument?

_____

_____

_____

Who is famous for playing this instrument?

_____

_____

_____

_____

XAI-XAI

Color this location on the map:

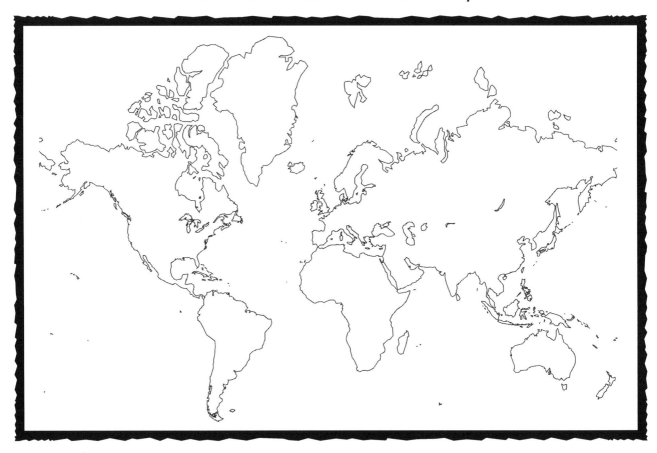

How far do you have to travel to reach this destination?
How would you get there?
What is the cost of travel to this location?
What is the currency called?
What is the current exchange rate?
What language is spoken there?
What is the weather like right now in this location?
What would you pack for this trip?

WRITE, DRAW OR PASTE A PHOTO

Flag	Popular Food
Current Events	Famous Landmark
A Famous Person	A Postage Stamp

TRY A TRADITIONAL RECIPE

Ingredients:

_____
_____
_____
_____
_____
_____
_____
_____
_____
_____
_____
_____
_____
_____
_____
_____
_____
_____

Prep Time:

Oven Temp:

Cook Time:

Directions:

_____
_____
_____
_____
_____
_____
_____
_____
_____
_____
_____
_____
_____
_____
_____
_____
_____
_____
_____
_____

Draw a picture or paste a photo of your culinary masterpiece here

FROM YOUR RESEARCH,
FIND & DEFINE 10 NEW SPELLING WORDS

1. xenodochial _____

_____

2. xerox _____

_____

3. _____

_____

4. _____

_____

5. _____

_____

6. _____

_____

7. _____

_____

8. _____

_____

9. _____

_____

10. _____

_____

CURSIVE PRACTICE
Copy the words on this page.
Use the next page to write
your spelling words in cursive.

Xander

xenodochial

xerus

plays

the

xylophone

in

Xai-Xai

FILM STUDY

Find a video about the animal, instrument, or place. Draw something from the video and share what you learned in the space provided below.

Name of Video: _____

Notes:

_____

_____

_____

_____

_____

_____

_____

_____

YURI THE YIELDING YAK PLAYS
THE YUNLUO IN YICHANG

MEET THE YAK

My scientific name:

_____

Where do I live?

_____

_____

What do I eat?

_____

_____

_____

Describe my home/habitat and behavior.

_____

_____

_____

_____

_____

_____

_____

Write about my history or folklore.

_____

_____

_____

_____

_____

ALL ABOUT THE YUNLUO

Describe this instrument.

_____
_____
_____
_____
_____
_____

Meaning of its name:

_____
_____

When, where, and by whom was it invented?

_____
_____
_____
_____

How do you play this instrument?

_____
_____
_____

Who is famous for playing this instrument?

_____
_____
_____
_____

YICHANG

Color this location on the map:

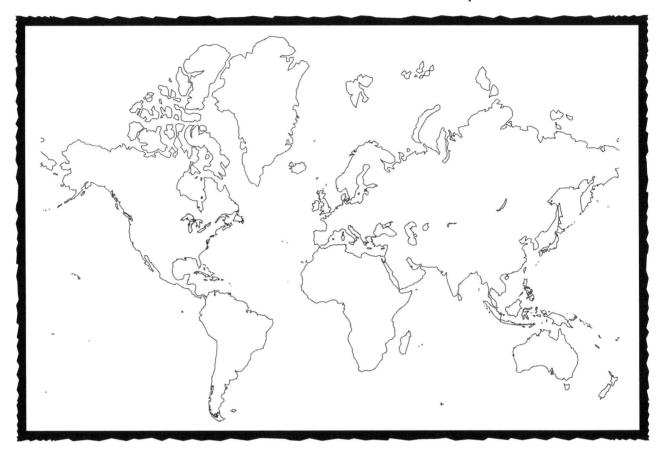

How far do you have to travel to reach this destination?
How would you get there?
What is the cost of travel to this location?
What is the currency called?
What is the current exchange rate?
What language is spoken there?
What is the weather like right now in this location?
What would you pack for this trip?

WRITE, DRAW OR PASTE A PHOTO

Flag	Popular Food
Current Events	Famous Landmark
A Famous Person	A Postage Stamp

DRAW OR PASTE PHOTOS OF TRADITIONAL CLOTHING

FROM YOUR RESEARCH,
FIND & DEFINE 10 NEW SPELLING WORDS

1. yielding _____

_____

2. yearn _____

_____

3. _____

_____

4. _____

_____

5. _____

_____

6. _____

_____

7. _____

_____

8. _____

_____

9. _____

_____

10. _____

_____

CURSIVE PRACTICE

Copy the words on this page.
Use the next page to write
your spelling words in cursive.

Yuri

yielding

yak

plays

the

yunluo

in

Yichang

Cursive Practice

A B C D E F G
H I J K L M
N O P Q R S T
U V W X Y Z

a b c d e f g h
i j k l m n o p
q r s t u v w x
y z 1 2 3 4 5 6 7 8 9 0

ZEKE THE ZESTFUL ZEBRA PLAYS THE ZITHER IN ZAMBIA

MEET THE ZEBRA

Where do I live?

_____

_____

What do I eat?

_____

_____

_____

_____

My scientific name:

_____

Describe my home/habitat and behavior.

_____

_____

_____

_____

_____

_____

_____

Write about my history or folklore.

_____

_____

_____

_____

_____

_____

ALL ABOUT THE ZITHER

Describe this instrument.

_____

_____

_____

_____

_____

_____

_____

Meaning of its name:

_____

_____

When, where, and by whom was it invented?

_____

_____

_____

_____

How do you play this instrument?

_____

_____

_____

_____

Who is famous for playing this instrument?

_____

_____

_____

_____

ZAMBIA

Color this location on the map:

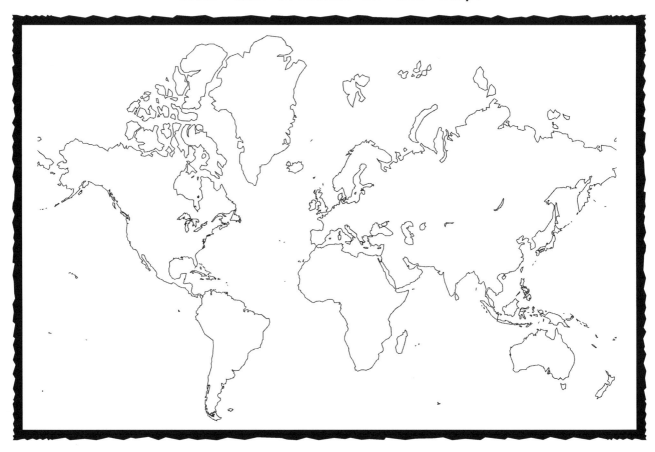

How far do you have to travel to reach this destination?
How would you get there?
What is the cost of travel to this location?
What is the currency called?
What is the current exchange rate?
What language is spoken there?
What is the weather like right now in this location?
What would you pack for this trip?

WRITE, DRAW OR PASTE A PHOTO

Flag	Popular Food

Current Events	Famous Landmark

A Famous Person	A Postage Stamp

WORD SEARCH FUN!

```
S M W D C J V W I R X F S J J K V I C U N A K
O U D I U W H P A S J E N U R U J K Y B X Y U
G T I R O A S M V R T A N I M L I W U Y C W L
R M Q H Y S U F E S M P X O U A G Z N E L L I
U Z Q E S H R L N Z I H J K D A C N L K X U S
B D N N U T E O E U Z V E Y W O K I U R A F E
S Y G I O U X W Z S Y A O A Z L C A O U N T S
F I N R R B S A U Q I W M A R E Q H R T D S F
L Y I U E B E K E T C T Z B D T K X I I E E X
O A D O F A L N L I H Q M B I O E E A A R Z G
W U L B I S E Y A G A T J G R A M D W I L A M
I G E M C S L L F E N B E N O H P O L Y X Q J
R U I A O B U O B R G R E H T I Z K A Y Y A U
U R Y T V D K V A S J N O K G A D E V I U I I
Y U Z Z O W U T W H A L U L L A T B A R B E Z
Y A N G G O W Q L V B H S I F L E S N U M S U
```

Find the following words in the puzzle.
Words are hidden ↑ ↓ → ← and ↘ .

TALLULAH	URUGUAY	WILMINA	YAK	ZESTFUL
TAMBOURINE	VEDA	WOLF	YICHANG	ZITHER
TIGER	VENEZUELA	WOLFSBURG	YIELDING	
TURKEY	VICUNA	XAIXAI	YUNLUO	
UAKARI	VOCIFEROUS	XANDER	YURI	
UKULELE	VOLYNKA	XENODOCHIAL	ZAMBIA	
ULISES	WARMHEARTED	XERUS	ZEBRA	
UNSELFISH	WASHTUBBASS	XYLOPHONE	ZEKE	

258

FROM YOUR RESEARCH,
FIND & DEFINE 10 NEW SPELLING WORDS

1. zestful _____

_____

2. zip _____

_____

3. _____

_____

4. _____

_____

5. _____

_____

6. _____

_____

7. _____

_____

8. _____

_____

9. _____

_____

10. _____

_____

CURSIVE PRACTICE
Copy the words on this page.
Use the next page to write
your spelling words in cursive.

Zeke

zestful

zebra

plays

the

zither

in

Zambia

WRITE A SHORT STORY, SONG, OR POEM USING THESE WORDS:

Zeke Zebra Zither
Zambia Zestful Zip

Title: _____   Date: _____

_____

_____

_____

_____

_____

_____

_____

_____

_____

_____

_____

Illustrate your story, song, or poem here

WORD SEARCH FUN!

```
F N K N G J O C H G H E Z I N O M R A H M B X
B D I R H W R W A S B U C O Z X E X O R E X U
I F N B A N I E X E F W S E E M T S J Y H C K
Y A D R R E G T H N H L Y Q N E A C B R V B T
N S L A E G I A N T O J J Y V Y A I E E O A D H
S C E N C O N V J I P X E E V S T T T E E E R
U I J D O T A I Y M L Y N N L U N A A T Z I I
J N H I M I T T F E T N R E B R E L N A E X V
M A R S M A E P A N B A U R Q E R U I R G Q E
J T W H E T A A L T O P O A X Q E T M E A U K
L E V U N E E C M A R M J T F Y F S U N R A B
P T F M D Y G F J L I O Y E F H F O L E U L N
B X Q F G Q N R P I A C Q U V I I P L G O I R
B C N Q T F U E Y Z P C W S L B D F I V C F A
D Q R J U M P I Z E W A O G R E D N U R N Y E
Q R Z V H C N U A L J E M O C L E W E Q E V Y
```

Find the following words in the puzzle.
Words are hidden ↑ ↓ → ← and ↘ .

ACCOMPANY
BRANDISH
CAPTIVATE
DIFFERENTIATE
ENCOURAGE
FASCINATE
GENERATE
HARMONIZE

ILLUMINATE
JOURNEY
KINDLE
LAUNCH
MEASURE
NEGOTIATE
ORIGINATE
POSTULATE

QUALIFY
RECOMMEND
SENTIMENTALIZE
THRIVE
UNDERGO
VENERATE
WELCOME
XEROX

YEARN'
ZIP

263

Animals & Instruments World Tour

EXTRA CREDIT ACTIVITIES

Remember, when completing these activities,

you are encouraged to write in cursive.

Be creative! Add photos or illustrations to your research.

Have fun!

CURRENT EVENTS

Extra! Extra! Read all about it!

You are the reporter! Choose your favorite country or city from the ones you studied in this book and research a current event. As you take notes in the space provided, keep in mind the "5 W's": Who, what, when, where, and why. Who was involved, what happened, when did it happen, where did it happen, and why did it happen. When you have finished taking your notes, write an article about the current event on the newspaper template provided. Don't forget to add a title and illustrations or photos.

NOTES:

_____

_____

_____

_____

_____

_____

_____

_____

_____

_____

The Thinking Tree Times

Issue: _____ **Date:** _____

VIRTUAL TOUR

Take a virtual tour of your favorite country or city studied in this book. Use the internet, books, videos, magazines, travel guides, etc. to plan your week-long tour. Decide where you will stay, what and where you will eat, and what you will see and do. On the following pages, write a travel journal entry for each day of your tour. What sights did you visit? What and where did you eat? What are your first impressions of this location? Record your favorite memories. Don't forget photos or illustrations. Add extra photos or illustrations to your scrapbook. Have fun and be creative!

My Virtual Tour
of:_____

Date: _____   Location: _____

_____

_____

_____

_____

_____

_____

_____

_____

_____

Date: _____   **Location:** _____
_____
_____
_____

_____
_____
_____
_____
_____

Date: _____   **Location:** _____
_____
_____
_____
_____
_____
_____

Date: _____   **Location:** _____
_____
_____
_____
_____
_____
_____
_____

Date: _____   **Location:** _____

_____

_____

_____

_____

_____

_____

_____

Date: _____   **Location:** _____

_____

_____

_____

_____

_____

_____

_____

Date: _____   **Location:** _____

_____

_____

_____

_____

_____

_____

_____

My Travel Scrapbook of:

_____

HISTORICAL EVENT

Research a historical event that took place in the country/city of your choice. Pretend that you have been tasked with writing an article for publication on *Wikipedia*. Gather your sources, take notes, and then write your article. Add a photo or illustration of this event. Make sure to list your references!

Notes:

_____

_____

_____

_____

_____

_____

_____

_____

_____

_____

_____

_____

_____

_____

_____

_____

_____

_____

_____

_____

_____

_____

_____

_____

_____

_____

_____

_____

_____

_____

_____

_____

_____

_____

_____

_____

_____

_____

_____

References:

_____

_____

_____

_____

Date:

Location:

Participants:

Outcome:

DESIGN YOUR OWN ZOO

Have you ever thought about designing your own zoo? If so, here is your chance! Using the list of animals that you studied in this journal, choose 7-10 that you would like to include in your mini zoo. Begin thinking about the kind of habitat and care that each animal will need in order to thrive in your zoo. Use your research and the following list of questions to help you design your habitats.

What kind of habitat will the animal need? For example, does it live underwater? If so, the habitat will need lots of water.

What is the animal's habitat like in the wild? How can you best recreate this in your zoo? Think about what features you might add to make it feel more like home.

What is the size of the animal? Does it prefer living alone or in a group? Does your animal prefer spending time on the ground or in a tree? How active is your animal? The answers to these questions will help determine the size of your habitat.

What kind of features will the habitat need in order for your animal to be comfortable and healthy? For example, the animal will need shelter, fresh water, and a place to keep cool when the weather is hot and warm when it is cold. What other elements are essential to the animal's well-being?

Visitors will come to see your animals! How can you set up the habitat so that visitors can see the animals but not be too much of a disturbance to them?

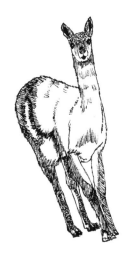

Animals need exercise and mental stimulation just like people do. What items could you add to the habitat that would keep them busy? Most animals forage for their food in the wild. How might you create a habitat that encourages this natural behavior? How could you feed them to create a challenge that keeps them active?

Obviously, there is much more that goes into creating a safe, healthy and comfortable habitat, but these questions will get you started. If you get stuck, go to a local zoo or look at zoo websites for photos of existing habitats to spark your creativity. Use the next 2 pages to begin taking notes and designing a habitat for one of your animals. You may photocopy these pages or use your own paper to design habitats for the rest of your zoo animals.

NOTES:

DRAW YOUR HABITAT!

Extra Credit: Make a 3D model of your habitat. Take a photo and

DRAW A MAP OF YOUR ZOO!

Use the space provided to draw a map of your zoo! Don't forget to include all your animal habitats and any other features you think are important.

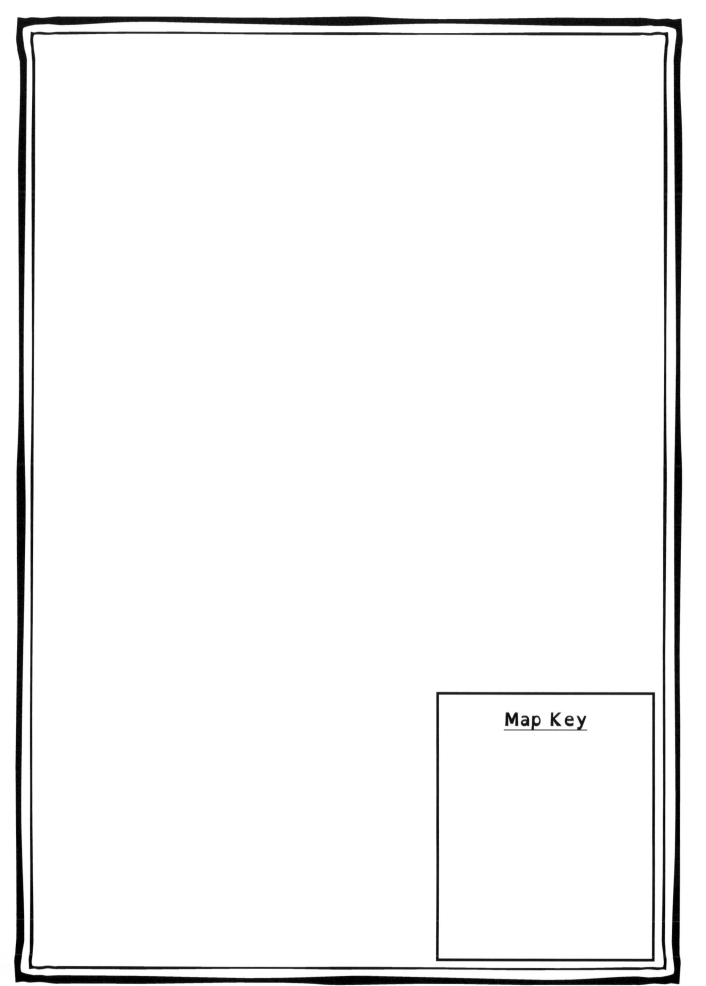

Map Key

Fun-Schooling With Thinking Tree Books

Copyright Information

Contact Us:

The Thinking Tree LLC

+1 (USA)   317.622.8852

info@funschooling.com

Learn more about Fun-Schooling at:

FunSchooling.com

Made in the USA
Monee, IL
20 February 2023

28300245R00155